Dance Like No One is Watching

THIS BOOK BELONGS TO

....

All rights reserved. No part of this publication may be reproduced, distributed, or transmitted in any form or by any means, including photocopying, recording, or other electronic or mechanical methods, without the prior written permission of the publisher.

Made in the USA
Middletown, DE
29 July 2020